TIME IN LIFE'S WAITING ROOM

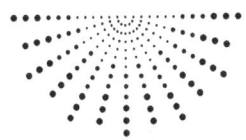

JOAN E. MURRAY

Book cover designed by, Woodson Creative Studio.

Joan Murray Ministries & Seeds Of Hope Worldwide Missions
26340 FM 1736
Waller, TX 77848
281-398-2501

CONTENTS

INTRODUCTION

Have you ever spent excessive time waiting for something you desperately wanted? Did you get frustrated because the wait was so long and tedious?

All of us have had seasons when we have waited for something special to manifest in our lives. During these seasons of waiting, we can become discouraged and give up hope our desires will ever be met. I believe the waiting season in a person's life is one of the most challenging times to go through because you cannot do anything to hurry the process.

You must wait, hope, and trust the outcome you believe will manifest at the right time in your life. The problem for you and me is the right time feels like right now, but it is not happening now.

"Why do we spend so much of our life waiting?"

In the waiting, you truly develop into the person God wants you to become. Your heart and life are qualified during the waiting season processes to determine whether God can use you in His Kingdom. The Bible says *those who wait upon the Lord will renew their strength; they will mount up with wings as eagles, run, and not get weary; walk, and not faint (Isaiah 40:31).*

As you read this scripture, you can see the waiting season is a time of equipping and preparation where you are getting stronger and maturing. This season develops courage that enables you to climb above the circumstances of life and teaches you how not to get tired as you wait for the promises to manifest.

When we get weary, we tend to give up, but as you wait, you become like Jesus, God's Son, who waited for thirty years to fulfill a three-year destiny. Although your future may be much longer, the time you spend waiting on God is to work out unnecessary things in your life that can stop you from fulfilling your purpose.

During the waiting season, God will develop His character and likeness in you; you will discover that being like His Son is the greatest gift you can receive. As God purifies, refines, develops, and equips you, you will become like the silver and gold – pure and ready to be used by Him. Your time in the waiting ensures you will reflect God to everyone you meet. When people see you, they will see a reflection of the King.

So, wait, do not get in a hurry! If your King has allowed you to be in a waiting season, trust He knows what is best for you. God has done this because your Creator wants time alone with you to know Him better.

Enjoy your time being processed and prepared for the Master's use.

Joan E. Murray

OTHER BOOKS BY AUTHOR

JOAN E. MURRAY

Boldness in Christ

Broken, Yet Unstoppable

Called and Chosen for Destiny

Discovering God Vol. 1

Discovering God Vol. 2

Faith That Conquers

Flow Through Me, Lord

Freedom In The Son

Hope In Difficult Seasons

I MUST PRAY

Lord, Make Me Whole

Overcoming Loneliness and Aloneness

Reconnect

Señor, Hazme Íntegro

Show Me How to Love

Time in Life's Waiting Room

Winning In The Battles of Life

Worship, Our Deepest Need

You Can TRUST Him

1

WHY AM I HERE?

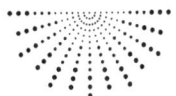

The question 'Why am I here?' is a question I have asked the Lord many times during my years of service to Him. I have spent most of my Christian life in the waiting room and have experienced intense struggles during the waiting seasons. I have struggled to keep the faith; maintain my peace; keep my joy and allow it to overflow. I had also struggled to stand and keep standing when all around me seemed as if it was dead or dying.

Though my time in the waiting room has been painful and hard at times, it has strengthened my character and deepened my faith. I am the first to tell you I would not have chosen to go through those intense seasons of waiting. I would have much preferred God to do things more quickly, but that was not His plan for me. As a result of my time in the waiting, I have discovered God has great plans for those who will allow Him to do the work in their lives that He desires to do. This work ensures your effectiveness in the assignments He wants you to fulfill.

Many of you are also asking the 'why' question. Why am I here? God, where are you? How long are you going to allow me to struggle and struggle? I pray the thoughts and sentiments expressed in this book will give you peace as you gracefully wait for God to act.

Understand God Has Placed You On His Schedule To Spend Time With Him In The Waiting Room.

God does some deep work in the waiting room as He prepares you for the assignments He has for your life. As He works on your heart, He starts by uprooting things that hinder your growth and keeping you from His best for you. King David experienced some intense waiting seasons, and he is a perfect example of how to wait, hope, and trust in the faithfulness of God.

Have mercy upon me, O God, according to thy loving kindness: according unto the multitude of thy tender mercies blot out my transgressions. Wash me thoroughly from mine iniquity, and cleanse me from my sin. For I acknowledge my transgressions: and my sin is ever before me. Against thee, thee only, have I sinned, and done this evil in thy sight: that thou mightest be justified when thou speakest, and be clear when thou judgest. Create in me a clean heart, O God; and renew a right spirit within me. Cast me not away from thy presence; and take not thy holy spirit from me.

Restore unto me the joy of thy salvation; and uphold me with thy free spirit.
Psalm 51:1-4; 10-12 (KJV)

Are you asking these questions, "Why am I here? Why am I in a waiting or holding pattern? Why does it seem I go from one difficult situation to another?" Then the answers to your questions are -- God is working on your heart and preparing you to be used by Him. He is also pruning unnecessary things from your life.

There will be seasons in your life when God begins to finalize His work in your heart and move you into the position He has ordained for you. Before He moves you, He will put you back on the potter's wheel and press unnecessary things out of your life so nothing will keep you from the assignments and blessings He has reserved for you. As God begins the work of developing your character, you will experience the pain of dying to self, selfish desires, and selfish ambitions.

The difficult situations you experience do not come from God — they are from the devil, but God will use these difficulties to form His character in you. You are in God's waiting room so He can purge, mold, make, and fashion you into His likeness. This time is necessary to get us into a deep, intimate relationship with Him.

In the waiting room, you may experience seasons of lack, sickness, relationship troubles, loneliness, sadness, depression, etc. You may wonder what is causing these problems and what you have done to deserve this. You did nothing to deserve it! The devil is trying to destroy the good work God has faithfully begun in you. The devil has caused these calamities, but he must have forgotten God will be glorified through your life. In every difficulty the devil brings your way, God *promises all things to work together for good to those who love God and those who are called according to His purpose (Romans 8:28).*

As I said, King David experienced many waiting room seasons in his life - times he had to wait, hope, pray, and trust the Lord. He often cried out to God for help. He taught us how to pour out our hearts to the only One who can help us. In the preceding passage of scripture, you can feel his pain and hear the deep cry of his heart to God. He began by petitioning God for mercy, reminding Him of His loving-kindness, and begging Him to wipe away his transgressions – sin, disobedience, crime, and violations – against Him.

David needed cleansing, and he asked God to cleanse him. He wanted to be washed, cleansed, and purified - to be clean through and through.

David's sin caused him to miss hearing God, miss the intimate relationship he had with Him, and he could no longer feel joy and gladness in his heart. David understood he was in a place of brokenness, and only God could heal and make him whole again. God's face and His presence were hidden from David because of sin. David repented and poured out his heart to God to get back into a right relationship with Him. He asked God to create a clean, unspotted heart in him and to renew a right spirit and attitude of the heart within him.

David remembered when King Saul sinned, God cast him away and took His Holy Spirit from him. The result was King

Saul being tormented by evil spirits. David begged God not to take the Holy Spirit from him because he did not want to go insane and lose his mind or life. He asked God to give him His salvation and freedom in the Spirit. David was in the waiting room, which was necessary because work needed to be done in his heart so he could accomplish more for God.

David was willing to go into the waiting room because he needed God and understood he could accomplish nothing without Him. He trusted in God!

When seeking the Lord and desiring to find out why I was in the waiting seasons, I realized God wanted to work in my heart as He did in David and many others in the Bible. His work in my heart was so He could do more significant work in and through my life.

In the waiting room, God begins to show you your true self. He begins to unveil the secret or hidden things because He wants you to be victorious. Sometimes these things keep us from having an intimate relationship with God because they may be unwholesome.

Some people have secret petitions that only God knows. These secret desires/petitions are so deep and painful that God must draw them close in the waiting room. Then He can begin healing their brokenness and unveiling His good-ness to them. King David experienced great brokenness in his life. In the waiting room, God not only mended his heart but caused greatness to arise within him. David was willing to endure the waiting room season to live in the fullness of joy.

David understood he would not attain much unless he allowed God to do the work in his life. He chose to endure this intense time of purging, cleansing, and preparation so God could be glorified through him.

When we are under pressure, many of us usually try to find a way to escape. What we fail to realize is being in the pressure cooker, at times, is necessary so we can maximize the full potential of God in our lives. Pressure has a way of bringing junk to the surface, and this allows us to live free from encumbrances. When we are free, we can be used to bring honor and glory to God. You are also in the waiting room so God can purge, cleanse, wash, mold, and make you. He is doing deep cleaning, which we will cover in an upcoming chapter.

Allow God to do the work so you can be effective for Him. Do not despise the waiting room, as this is where you get to spend time alone with God. When He is finished with you, your life will be changed and transformed forever.

2

THE REFINER'S FIRE

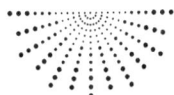

The purpose of being refined is to be purified and cleansed, better educated, improve our character, and make us more extraordinary. During the waiting season, we are refined as we learn to hope, trust, walk by faith, and believe in God for breakthroughs. This refining is done so we can reflect the Lord Jesus Christ to a world that needs to encounter Him. Let us look at a few scriptures to see what God says about being refined.

But who may abide the day of his coming? And who shall stand when he appeareth? For he is like a refiner's fire, and like a fullers' soap: And he shall sit as a refiner and purifier of silver: and he shall purify the sons of Levi, and purge them as gold and silver, that they may offer unto the LORD an offering in righteousness.
Malachi 3:2-3 (KJV)

And I will bring the third part through the fire, and will refine them as silver is refined, and will try them as gold is tried: they shall call on my name, and I will hear them: I will say, It is my people: and they shall say, The LORD is my God.
Zechariah 13:9 (KJV)

The answer to the question "How is silver refined?" is essential because it will be the springboard used to share the process God takes each of us through as He prepares us for His assignments.

Pure silver is seldom found outside of a jewelry store. Impure silver is all around, and those impurities can easily be refined if one takes all the necessary precautions. Refining silver without using a large smelting oven requires using nitric acid. Safety is still as important, if not more so than it would be when using a smelting oven. It takes one hundred and fifty ML of concentrated nitric acid for every ounce of metal to be purified. Nitric acid is extremely acidic and can cause permanent damage if it comes in contact with a person's skin. The use of safety gear is of paramount importance.

After the silver is put into a bucket, it is weighed, and the appropriate amount of nitric acid is added. The silver will react violently to the acid, foaming, and bubbling for several minutes as it dissolves. The bucket should only be one-third full of metal before pouring the acid into it. Periodically, the contents must be stirred to speed up the dissolving process. You must wait for the silver to dissolve into the acid completely and for the acid to stop bubbling and foaming. When the reaction stops, the bucket contents are poured through a filter into another bucket. The filter prevents the impurities left behind from escaping into the second bucket.

You must closely follow the instructions to get the results and not harm yourself. Any deviation will result in serious bodily injury, which can apply to our waiting room seasons. We must allow God to work a thorough process in our hearts to get the best results and be willing to leave the impurities behind.

During our refining process, we often feel like someone has dropped us into an unbearable acidic situation. When put into a challenging situation, we might react negatively, even aggressively, as the silver reacts violently when the acid is poured onto it. This pressure cooker, this refiner's fire, this waiting season you are in, is designed to cause the best of who you are to rise to the surface. However, to get to the core of who you are means God must go beyond the impurities in your life.

As He begins this work, you may feel the pain and pressure as it builds and builds until you feel as if you are going to explode. Now, you must decide what you are going to do.

Are you going to be brutally honest with yourself and determine you will do whatever it takes to be who God wants you to be? Will you allow God to do the deep work in your heart? Or will you abort the process because it is too painful? If we are honest with ourselves, many of us have given up because we were unwilling to go through the intense work necessary to bring about our healing and freedom.

Over the years, I have spent time in various hospital waiting rooms as a patient or visiting someone. I have observed people as they waited for the results or report from the doctor. Some are agitated, others are worried and stressed, and on a few occasions, I found some prayerful and peaceful as they waited. What has stood out the most, however, is how few of us handle life's struggles with grace. Some of us have not found the sustaining peace of God during our difficulties. The fire has been heated up in our lives; we feel like we are swimming upstream. It seems as if the bottom has fallen out of our world. We cannot find comfort because the problems appear so great.

Even believers in desperate situations have often taken our eyes off the ultimate Caregiver. We are so focused on the problem –what one can do in difficult situations – we have not yet realized God is with us. We often make the problem bigger than God and forget the promises in the Word of God – He would be with us, bring us through the fire, and when we call, He will hear and answer.

God says when you pass through the waters, I will be with you; and through the rivers, they shall not overflow you: when you walk through the fire, you shall not be burned; neither shall the flame scorch you
Isaiah 43:2.

Unfortunately, during a crisis, our minds are clouded with anxious thoughts, and we forget the Word. It is hard to believe God is with us during turbulent times. When we feel the heat of the fire, we are sure we will burn, but God says otherwise.

Let me remind you that you serve a God who cannot lie.

His nature is the Truth, so He *must* fulfill what He has promised. Here is scripture worth memorizing.

Numbers 23:19 says, *God is not a man, that he should lie, nor a son of man, that he should change his mind. Does he speak and then not act? Does he promise and not fulfill?*

As you meditate on this scripture, you must reach your conclusions by answering God's questions. As you go through adversity, you can find hope and comfort in the Word.

As I said, many of us have asked the 'why me' questions. What have I done to deserve this? Why is God allowing this to happen to me? Why has God abandoned me? The painful seasons of waiting are trying, and we cry out for answers in our brokenness. I have noticed people who do not believe in God will also cry out to Him for answers. We cry out to Him because God created within us an 'inner knowledge' that He is available to us. When life becomes unbearable, even those who say they do not believe in God will reach out to Him because deep down, they know He exists.

Think about this with me; did Jesus do anything to deserve to endure such suffering and horrific death? Not! He was perfect and sinless, yet He suffered greatly. God did not exempt Him from any trials and testing. Jesus endured pain and suffering so He could relate to us. As a result, He reminds God to pardon us when we sin and miss His high standards. Sometimes our suffering is caused by bad decisions and choices. When this occurs, God's grace is sufficient to help us as we walk through the consequences. At other times we are attacked by the enemy and have done nothing to deserve such pain and suffering. God is aware of where we are; He knows what to do to relieve our suffering. Remember, God is your Father, and He is not unkind or a mean Father. He loves you and is compassionate even when you may be at fault.

In the book of Job, Job endured some hard times even though he was a righteous man. God allowed these trials in Job's life because, like Jesus, there was more incredible fruit that would come forth through his trials. Although Job opened the door through fear, the devastation Satan brought into his life was immense. Yet Job did not let go of God during His troubles; he overcame and was victorious. You can read more about Job's story in my book, **Winning in the Battles of Life.**

When you encounter devastating situations, remember the Word of God, and having done all, to stand (Ephesians 6:13). Stand and pray, stand in faith, hope, and trust in the faithfulness of God. When we go through the refiner's fire, all the impurities in our hearts are brought to the surface. It lets us see we need God's power to help us live wholesome and pure lives. Without God's power working through us, our lives can become unmanageable, pointless, and mediocre. God is weeding out the harmful things that have entangled many of us and keep us from maximizing our potential in Him.

When we are in the fires of adversity, it is painful, and we may feel hopeless. Joy will return. You hope God will see you through and bring you out with great power.

Too few of us will allow God to refine our characters so He can use us for His greater good. We want the many blessings He bestows but do not want to go through the hard and challenging places to receive them. If Jesus had not willingly suffered and died, we would not be enjoying our freedom today. He had a choice about allowing God to refine Him. Remember in the Garden of Gethsemane when Jesus asked for the cup to be removed from Him? He was feeling the pressure about what He would face, not only on the cross but the sufferings He would endure before it. We are glad He quickly told God it was not about His will and doing His own thing, but God's will would be accomplished in His life (Matthew 26:39).

In the waiting seasons, God is glorified as we trust and hope in His unfailing love and promises. So, are you now willing and ready to let God refine you? When He takes you through this refining process, you can be assured that He knows what is best for you and can see the fantastic outcome for your life. As you have trusted Him with your eternal salvation, you can trust Him to work in you because the result will be an abundant harvest in your life. He will walk you through the refining process.

3

FORMED INTO THE IMAGE OF THE SON

Change is continually taking place in your life because God wants you to look like His Son, Jesus. He is molding you into His likeness and image and showing you His way of doing and being. The word form means to shape, configure, make, construct, build, trim, and to cut. God is reshaping your life to take you from sinfulness to holiness. He is reconstructing and rebuilding His character in you. He will trim and cut away what is unnecessary, so you reflect His likeness to others.

Jesus also spent time in the waiting room while on earth as a man. For thirty years, He waited to fulfill the assignment God gave him. We ask, "Why did God allow Jesus to wait thirty years?" Possibly for the same reason He allows you to wait. Those unwilling to do what God wants them to do are flushed out.

In the waiting, God begins to do thorough work in your life and points out things not conducive to the assignment

He has given you. Some of these are rebellion, bitterness, unforgiveness, frustration, and a lack of willingness to follow where God leads. These things will surface as we struggle and wait, and they can be considered hindrances to fulfilling our assignments.

God uses the waiting seasons to temper our hearts and remold us into His Son's likeness.

God used the waiting season in Jesus' life to train, equip, mold, and make Him into the perfect example we could emulate and pattern our lives after. He was victorious over sin! As I think about how God allowed His Son, Jesus, to wait such a long time to fulfill only a three-year destiny, I am amazed at how much God loves us.

God allowed Jesus to patiently wait on His perfect timing to fulfill His plan of redemption. Jesus had to be tested, tempted and tried. He had to face and overcome our enemy, the devil, so He could be the perfect example of how to be victorious when we come face-to-face with the enemy. He went through the testing without sinning and demonstrated how to gain victory with the help of the Holy Spirit. Jesus taught us how to live free from the enemy's entrapment and to glorify and honor God in everything we do.

Not only did Jesus live free from sin, but He also showed us how, after God fashions us into His image, we can become a true reflection and example of Him. Galatians 5:22-26 says,

"But the fruit of the Spirit is love, joy, peace, long-suffering, gentleness, goodness, faith, meekness, temperance; against such there is no law. And they that are Christ's have crucified the flesh with the affections and lusts. If we live in the Spirit, let us also

walk in the Spirit. Let us not be desirous of vainglory, provoking one another, envying one another."

This is a clear picture of who Jesus is, how He lived, and how He was able to conquer the devil and bring us freedom. He operated in the fruit of the Spirit, and love was His motivation for everything He did. Along with His great love was His powerful example of how Believers should operate in the fruit of the Spirit, which brings success. Jesus used the Word to defeat the enemy, and we must also use God's Word to attain victory.

What would exempt us from our waiting season if the Son of God had to wait a long time to fulfill His assignment? As we become formed into His image, we will bear fruit representing God's Kingdom. This fruit will fill our lives with the peace of God and will remain in us throughout eternity.

I am crucified with Christ: nevertheless I live; yet not I, but Christ liveth in me: and the life which I now live in the flesh I live by the faith of the Son of God, who loved me, and gave himself for me. I do not frustrate the grace of God.
Galatians 2:20-21a (KJV)

The scripture begins with a bang - I am crucified – I am dead! The Apostle Paul shares what it takes to be formed into the image of Christ. You must be crucified with Him. You must experience death to yourself. This means death to your hopes, wishes, and desires, enabling you to live fully for Christ's desires and wishes. In Jesus' crucifixion, He bore all our sins, shame, and pain. They were all nailed to the cross, allowing us to overcome and be conquerors.

To be crucified with Him means you realize your life can only be lived by Him, for Him, and through Him. As you live from day to day, trust Him to meet your needs and to support you when life gets hard. You can trust Him because He gave His all for you; therefore, He will not withhold anything good from you. His love for you caused Him to give His life so you may enjoy your life.

Part of being conformed to the image of Jesus is being careful how you use the grace He has freely given you. Grace is unearned favor, and we did not earn it because of our goodness and did not deserve it. We have all sinned and fallen short of God's standards.

God decided to pour His grace on us because His sinless Son took our punishment, allowing us to experience His forgiveness and grace.

Galatians 2:21 issues a challenge for you and me. It tells us not to frustrate the grace of God. This means – don't thwart, nullify, hinder, circumvent, and defeat God's grace in our lives. We must let go of all habitual sin to keep from frustrating God's grace. Many people continually sin because they understand God promises to forgive them when they do sin. However, they have neglected to realize that God sees the motives of their hearts. He knows our sincerity, and when we confess 1 John 1:9, *"If we confess our sins, He is faithful and just to forgive us our sins, and to cleanse us from all unrighteousness,"* God knows if we are only giving Him lip service or whether we are genuine.

He knows if we intend to return to sin as soon as we feel

better. Since He knows these things, let me pose a few questions, "Does God know when our confession is not sincere? Are we forgiven if we do not intend to turn away from the sin?" I encourage you to get alone with God and find the answers to these questions, so you will know where you stand in your relationship with Him.

God is looking for people whose hearts are fixed on Him. Those who know and love God will seek to obey Him. The Bible tells us if we love Him, we will keep His commandments (John 14:15). Remember all God has given us through the life and death of His Son – His love, grace, mercy, and forgiveness. The Son gave us – His love, heart, pardon, and life. The Holy Spirit gives us comfort, and He defends and leads us. You have all you need in the Father, Son, and Holy Spirit to live a victorious Christian life. God will mold you into the image of the One who is so precious, Jesus. You can trust God!

Choose to be reformed, reshaped, reconfigured, remade, reconstructed, rebuilt, trimmed, and then cut into the image of the Son.

4

FASHIONED FOR KINGDOM WORK

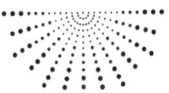

The time you have already spent or will spend in the waiting room is the time when God begins to fashion you for work in His Kingdom. This time with God helps you tune in to what He wants to do with your life. In **Called and Chosen for Destiny**, we talked about how God has given each person a destiny only they are qualified to fulfill.

There are no substitutes in the Kingdom; your assignment was chosen for you and placed in your heart before you were formed in your mother's womb. God preplanned how you would use your life to glorify Him. This means you were fashioned for a specific assignment in the Kingdom. This assignment was given to you because God has given you the necessary gifts to fulfill it. As you spend time in the waiting room, God begins to mold your will and desire to line up with His. The fashioning He does in your heart is to direct you away from any path that will take you from where He wants you to be.

Have you ever gone to visit someone more than once but chose to use a different route? This new direction got you to the destination, but there were some new observations along the way. Sometimes, it took a little longer to get where you were going. You were distracted by the new things you saw and spent extra time trying to absorb it all.

If God does not fashion us for our Kingdom assignments, we will make many detours that will delay or even cause us to go off course. Some people encounter challenges and other opportunities along the way and never arrive at their destination. Some roadblocks are placed in our path by the enemy. Those roadblocks will keep us from connecting with the right people and obtaining our blessings if we are not careful. These roadblocks can be distractions designed to entice us away from God's plan, and they can also be troubling situations we must work through.

Over the years, I have studied people who appear to be fulfilling the plan of God for their lives. Sometimes they experience a crisis with their family, job, or relationship, and as they rush in to fix the problem, they get lost and go off course. These crises can also help fashion us for Kingdom work if we only believe God can give us the solutions to the problems. It is sad to say, but many people do not seek Him in their crisis, so they do not receive the answers.

At times, our problems can be so overwhelming we might forget we are on a journey and become stuck where we are. For God to fashion you for Kingdom assignments, you must be quick to hear and obey what He is saying. You must also be willing to follow even when unsure if you are qualified for this task. As God attempted to tell the Prophet Jeremiah about his Kingdom assignment, he had some challenges, and I pray you will find the solutions for your life in his story.

Then the word of the LORD came unto me, saying: Before I formed you in the belly I knew thee; and before thou camest forth out of the womb I sanctified thee, and I ordained thee a prophet unto the nations. Then said I, Ah, Lord GOD! behold, I cannot speak: for I am a child. But the LORD said unto me, Say not, I am a child: for thou shalt go to all that I shall send thee, and whatsoever I command thee thou shalt speak. Be not afraid of their faces: for I am with thee to deliver thee, saith the LORD. Then the LORD put forth his hand, and touched my mouth. And the LORD said unto me, Behold, I have put my words in thy mouth.
Jeremiah 1:4-9 (KJV)

Jeremiah's story paints a vivid picture of our work in the Kingdom. His story shows us God has a call for every life. When God calls you, He is calling forth the assignment He placed in your heart before you were formed in your mother's womb. God told Jeremiah before forming him; that He knew who he was. God is saying He created Jeremiah and all of us with a destiny. Therefore, after forming us, He fashions and molds us into what He designed us to be.

God told Jeremiah that He called him to be a prophet to the nations. Jeremiah responded quickly, as do many of us when the Lord begins to reveal what He has in mind for our lives. He told God he could not speak, yet it is evident he was conversing with God, so there was nothing wrong with his voice box. He told God he felt unqualified, untrained, and not fully equipped to be a prophet. He also told God he was a child, meaning, "Don't give me such a hard assignment."

The Lord responded by rebuking him, "Don't say you are a child and don't tell Me you can't do this work because you are not qualified. I have equipped you, and you are qualified for the task ahead of you." Does this sound familiar to you? Has God also corrected your wrong assumptions about yourself? How often have you told God you cannot do what He has asked you to do? God would not give you the assignment if He did not choose, destined, and qualify you for it.

Do you remember in the book of Genesis when God said, *"Let Us make man in Our image and likeness?"* God did not make you an inferior copy of Himself but made you like Him. This means God has given you His creative power and abilities and put all the necessary ingredients in your heart to produce the right results. When He begins talking to you about destiny, He is only attempting to awaken what He has already put in you. You will be secure in the knowledge God knows your capabilities. As He fashions you, you will begin to discover there are some hidden treasures within you. God knows everything, and He knows what you were born to accomplish - with that destiny in mind.

As God dealt with Jeremiah's uncertainty, He did not give him the option of running away. He told him he would go where he was sent and would speak the exact words God had given to him. He then addressed the core problem in Jeremiah's heart – fear. He was fearful of what the people would say. Jeremiah lived among them and was aware they were breaking God's laws and living sinful lives. He understood his task would not be easy, so he decided to walk away from his assignment. God gave him the same promise He has given to you – I am with you to deliver you!

You must make decisions as God begins to fashion you for Kingdom work. Some of you will tell the Lord you are unqualified, and the enemy will remind you of your past mistakes to convince you that no one will listen to you. God knows what He is doing, and He alone understands the impact you will make in many people's lives. He has called, qualified, equipped, and will train you for the work ahead.

See, I have this day set thee over the nations and over the kingdoms, to root out, and to pull down, and to destroy, and to throw down, to build, and to plant. Moreover the word of the LORD came unto me, saying, Jeremiah, what seest thou? And I said, I see a rod of an almond tree. Then said the LORD unto me, Thou hast well seen: for I will hasten my word to perform it. And the word of the LORD came unto me the second time, saying, what seest thou? And I said, I see a seething pot; and the face thereof is toward the north. Then the LORD said unto me, Out of the north an evil shall break forth upon all the inhabitants of the land. For, lo, I will call all the families of the kingdoms of the north, saith the LORD; and they shall come, and they shall set everyone on his throne at the entering of the gates of Jerusalem, and against all the walls thereof round about, and against all the cities of Judah.
Jeremiah 1:10-15 (KJV)

Jeremiah's story continues to be a prime example of how God prepares us for Kingdom work. After God dealt with his fear by calming his anxieties, God touched his mouth and put His words directly into it. Then God prophesied over Jeremiah's life the destiny he was called to fulfill. After God finished the prophecy, He tested Jeremiah to determine what he had seen, and Jeremiah replied he had seen a rod of an almond tree.

Let me share a little history to give you a picture of what God did for Jeremiah as He fashioned him for Kingdom work.

In Numbers chapter seventeen, the Israelites complained about Moses and Aaron because of their difficulties on their journey. They began to question both Moses' and Aaron's authority. The Lord was fed up and about to destroy them with a plague. Moses instructed Aaron to take a censer filled with incense and fire from the altar of God and run through the crowd of people to stop the plague. Even though Aaron moved quickly and ran into the midst of the people with the censer, fourteen thousand seven hundred died instantly.

God provided a solution to their murmuring and complaining. The following day, God told Moses to take one rod from each leader of the twelve tribes, including one from Aaron. Moses was to write the names of each leader on his rod and then place them in the tabernacle. God told him the rod of the man He would choose would blossom, and this would cause the people to stop complaining against His chosen leaders.

In the morning, Aaron's rod had not only budded and blossomed but also yielded almonds. After each man looked at his rod and saw it was unchanged, Aaron's rod was brought out. When the people saw it, they feared for their lives, and God showed them Aaron was His choice as leader.

When God asked Jeremiah what he saw, Jeremiah told Him he saw a rod of an almond tree. God told him he was right and was chosen to be His prophet. Jeremiah understood as God had used Aaron, God would also use him. God commended him for seeing the vision clearly and promised He would hasten His word to perform it in his life.

You have been given a promise. God has chosen you, placed His stamp of approval on your life, and marked you for His use. You will be equipped and trained for the Kingdom work. As you spend time with Him in the waiting room, as Jeremiah did, He will teach you to trust, obey, and depend on Him; He will help you fulfill your life's calling. God will touch your mouth and fill it with His words. He will speak through you and cause others to witness that you are His choice. God will hasten His Word to perform it in your life, and not one of His words concerning you will fail. He will mold and fashion you for Kingdom work. God can be trusted to finish what He started in you!

5
DEEP CLEANING

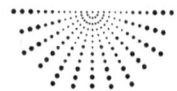

*H*ave you ever spent any time thoroughly cleaning your home? You cleaned the windows and baseboards, dusted every corner, cleaned the appliances, and vacuumed the entire house. You did this because you wanted your home to be thoroughly cleaned, and you desired your home to be spotless and fresh smelling. When God begins deep cleaning your heart, He also goes after everything. God wants to make your heart spotless and ensure you are refreshed in all areas of your life. God begins His work by looking at your heart to see what is hidden there, and then He begins to do deep cleaning so you can glorify Him with your life.

God begins by using His Word to purge wrong thoughts from your mind so your thoughts can be pure and wholesome. He then goes after the foods you feed your body (His temple) to ensure they will benefit your health. He sees what you listen to and what you allow to enter your eyegate and

He hears the words you speak. In all this, God is cleaning deep to prepare you for greatness. He intends to purge and purify your temple to make it a pure place where His Holy Spirit can dwell.

One of the most important times you will spend in God's waiting room is when you allow Him to do this deep work in you. This profound work is the preparation you need before being used by God. As He works, He is preparing you to be a clean and holy vessel that will bring Him glory and be used as a reflection of Himself to the world. Countless people in the world are looking for God, and many of them will only find Him as they look at those of us who profess to be Christians. Based on what they know or have heard about God, they will look at our example to decide if God is someone they can trust. Therefore, as Believers, we must make sure we are mature in Him, and we not only look the part but live as He lived. This does not mean we have to be perfect, but rather that we know and live by His Word. I invite you to look with me at the following scripture and assess where you are in your walk with God.

When I was a child, I spoke and thought and reasoned as a child. But when I grew up, I put away childish things. Now we see things imperfectly, like puzzling reflections in a mirror, but then we will see everything with perfect clarity. All that I know now is partial and incomplete, but then I will know everything completely, just as God now knows me completely.
1 Corinthians 13:11-12 (NLT)

As I reflect on the many seasons of deep cleaning I have experienced in the presence of the Lord, sometimes, it has been hard and challenging. During the process, my flesh screamed because it was being crucified. I had to let go of things I wanted to do even though I realized they were not right for me. Let me share some of those experiences with you because I believe some of you have had similar ones. One of my favorite hobbies is reading. I have loved reading since childhood but was not always selective about what I read. I love to read novels, and as some of you can attest, the content of many of these books does not glorify God or uplift anyone. The Lord began to deal with me about consecrating my eyes to Him, and he asked me to watch what I read and allow it to go from my eyes into my heart. When He began talking to me about what I read, He was also dealing with me about what I watched on television and at the movies. He asked me to stop watching things that were sexual, violent, magical, unholy, and impure.

What does that sound like to you? Does it appear God was telling me there was not much I could watch on television? Exactly! You can understand why it took me some time to let go of these things. Letting go of the unwholesome television shows and movies was much easier than letting go of books. Letting go of the novels took a few years longer because of my love for reading. Why do you think God asked this of me? There are several reasons – I am a believer; I had been asking Him to clean up my life, purify my temple, and fill me with more of Himself. I also asked Him to use me mightily in His Kingdom and for His glory. Before this could occur, you can see why deep cleaning was necessary.

One day I watched a movie on regular television, and the film's first thirty minutes seemed fine to me. About that time, I heard the still, small voice of the Holy Spirit asking me if I was going to continue watching it. I responded, telling Him I did not see anything wrong with the movie, and He said, "Look again," - sure enough, the scene had drastically changed. I struggled to turn the movie off because I like to know how a story ends. I had to get up from my seat, turn the TV off, and then occupy myself with something else to avoid disobeying the Holy Spirit and go back to watching the movie. I struggled with my fleshly desire to finish watching the movie even though the content was not conducive to what I wanted from the Lord.

God was doing a deep cleaning. He was answering my prayer so He could use me for His glory. He had begun the work by refining my character and desires and was intent on removing every unwholesome thing from my life, but I was not cooperating. I was fighting against the changes He wanted to implement.

Letting go of the things we momentarily enjoy can be challenging. We often justify our decisions by saying other Christians are doing those things. God is working on you, so you should not compare your life with someone else's. Keep in mind the work God is doing in your heart is for your benefit and not the benefit of others. Some people may see the changes in you, which might affect their lives and precipitate some changes in them. As we mature in the Lord and let go of childish things, we are better able to be a witness to others, for Him. Our childish ways do not bring honor and praise to God, so we must decide to grow up in Him.

When God completes His cleansing work in you, it will bring Him the most incredible honor and the highest glory. He will also abundantly bless you for your obedience, sacrifice, and willingness to follow His lead. The scripture reference in 1 Corinthians 13:12 tells us that we do not see things perfectly or clearly and view things through a cloudy mirror. Our view is unclear and foggy, but God wants us to see clearly. He wants us to look honestly at our hearts, lives, and motives and ask, "Am I bringing glory to God in my current condition?" What you and I currently have is only partial knowledge, and we do not have the complete picture because God has not yet revealed all things to us.

A day is coming when we know everything, and then we will understand why God requires us to crucify our flesh, die to ourselves, and live only for Christ. God understands you and knows your heart and desires because He created you. He knows what will cause you to be wounded and hurt, to fall and ultimately fail, so He tries to lead you down His path before the enemy can come in and derail your life.

When you and I look into the mirror of our lives, we often don't see ourselves as we are but through rose-tinted glasses. God asks us to take a close and honest look at our lives to see if we represent Him by how we live and conduct ourselves. God wants us to see ourselves clearly, and He wants us to decide we need His help to live a wholesome life. God is telling us when He looks at our hearts, some of them are clouded by wrong thoughts, ideas, and desires. Once we take a good, honest look, He invites us to enter His waiting room so the cleansing process can begin. God wants to work out those things in us that concern Him, and which will keep us from running our race in victory.

The deep cleaning is not only for our benefit but also for the benefit of those whom God has called us to help. God goes after the deep things in our lives because He does not want us to miss a single blessing, and God does not want us to live eternity separated from Him. Take a deep and careful look at your life and be honest with yourself by asking these questions:

What does God see when He looks at me?
Am I sold out to God?
Am I living in purity?
Do I satisfy my desires instead of God's?
Can God use me to bring glory to Himself?
Am I a good reflection of God to other people?
Is God pleased or displeased with me?
What can I do to keep the sacrifice of Jesus?
from having been in vain in my life?
How can I devote my life to pleasing Jesus because of
all He has done for me?
Do I truly trust Him?

Now, ask the Holy Spirit to lead you into the waiting room so God can begin the deep cleaning He needs to do in your heart. If you are afraid, say, "Holy Spirit, help me!" As you pray, He will guide you and provide all the help you need to be victorious in this season of deep cleaning. He will be with you!

6

LEAVE THE BAGGAGE

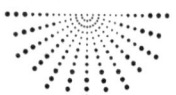

Years ago, I traveled often, and my suitcase was often cumbersome. During the first few years of traveling, I would take too many outfits and far too many pairs of shoes in case I might need them. As you realize, I was carrying unnecessary baggage because I could only wear a couple of outfits on each trip and never wore the extra ones.

After hauling so much baggage around for several years, it became heavy, burdensome, and difficult for me to transport. I eventually used good judgment and decided to leave the unnecessary baggage home. My load was tremendously lightened and made traveling much more fun.

We often carry unnecessary baggage because we think it is necessary and later find out it only weighs us down. Many of us, however, have carried emotional baggage throughout our lives. This baggage has kept us from being our true selves. It has also hindered us from attaining the fullness of our destinies. Sometimes, because of our baggage, we have made some bad decisions.

Come unto me, all ye that labor and are heavy laden, and I will give you rest. Take my yoke upon you and learn of me; for I am meek and lowly in heart: and ye shall find rest unto your souls. For my yoke is easy, and my burden is light.
Matthew 11:28-30 (KJV)

Many of you carry unnecessary baggage from your childhood, broken relationships; stresses on the job, and broken hearts. God wants you to leave the baggage and never intended you to bear these burdens. Through the death of His Son, God provided help for you if you are weighed down with the cares of life.

Some of you experienced an abusive, unhealthy, and painful childhood. The enemy uses these memories to keep you weighed down, and he tells you how others have experienced better lives than you. He reminds you of these things because he does not want you free to enjoy the good life and provisions Jesus died to give you. He convinces you to believe that you have no value and have been abused, abandoned, and neglected because you deserve it.

Let me proclaim it loud and clear - you did not deserve any negative things you experienced growing up! The enemy has designed them to either take your life or leave you broken so that you will haul this baggage for the rest of your days. People who abuse others also carry their baggage and add to their load each time they abuse another. They harm others because they are broken. Until God controls their lives and does a deep cleaning of their souls, their baggage will haunt them and keep them living mediocre, unhealthy lives.

Forgiveness is the key to freedom from those who have harmed you.

Forgiveness for the offender frees you to live your life without being hampered with unnecessary loads. When we choose not to forgive others, we are the ones who are ultimately hurt. Forgiveness breaks the hold an abusive person may have over you because you have released them. Remember, God says vengeance is His, and He will repay the offender (Romans 12:19). You don't have to fight this war by yourself because God is fully aware of the circumstances, and He will fight and win on your behalf.

This scripture says to come unto Him all who are downtrodden, and He will give you rest. He cannot provide rest if you will not go and share your pain and broken heart with Him. Some may be wondering where He was during the time you were suffering. He was right there attempting to reach the abuser and get them to stop, but their will overrode His desires. He was sheltering you and weeping with you during your struggles. He did not abandon you. During your most difficult times, God is always near.

Others have been crushed in relationships – friendships, marriages, and families. These situations are also meant to keep you from enjoying the abundant life Jesus died to give you. They are intended to make you feel worthless and hopeless. The enemy wants to keep you bogged down under the weight of your emotions, so your life becomes unbearable and not worth living.

I believe the enemy has caused these painful situations because he wants to keep you from God's best. The enemy knows when you leave the heavy baggage, you will do untold damage to his kingdom by sharing your testimony and helping others break free from their bondage.

We have all faced difficulties which have made us better or more bitter. Some of you have come out of your negative situations fighting mad and have used that energy to help fight for others. We have birthed great destinies and charities out of our difficulties and brought awareness to these areas. What was intended to cripple us has turned into our finest moment. Someone said without a test; there is no testimony. Some of you have used the severity of the trials and become more than conquerors. You have triumphed in the face of the enemy each time you share your struggles and victories with others in the same predicament.

Some of you struggle in school or work with your bosses and co-workers, while others struggle in day-to-day friendships. In all these situations, you may ask yourself, "Why me?" You may have low self-esteem or self-worth because you have trouble understanding why people do not accept you as you are. As a result, you are filled with pain, feel hopeless, lost, and alone, and might think you do not have a friend in the world. Jesus has a word of encouragement for you – *He is a friend that sticketh closer than a brother* (Proverbs 18:24). He is near to you and hears each time you pray.

Jesus called Abraham His friend; since you are Abraham's

son or daughter, you are also a friend of God. God will never leave you, forsake you, or abandon you. He is always with you to comfort, heal, deliver, and set you free of the baggage you have carried for years. His freedom brings joy, hope, encouragement, and love into your heart.

The baggage you have carried was meant to keep you from realizing the great King of the universe is deeply in love with you. He loves you so much; if you were the only person on earth, He would have still sent Jesus to die that horrible death for you! He loves you deeply! He is fighting for you! You can never be alone because His presence lives in you! He walks and talks with you and waits to have an audience with you each day. Therefore, if this great King considers you to be so unique and valuable, what do the opinions of mere men and women mean to you?

His opinion of you far exceeds all others.

Someone wants to free you of your baggage – He is God! His love for you carried a hefty price tag - the death of His beloved Son, Jesus. Let us hear what Jesus says since He knows you are burdened with life's cares.

Matthew chapter eleven tells us Jesus wants us to come to Him with all our worries, cares, burdens, and loads. He does not want you to keep laboring under the weight of your problems because you are not designed to handle them. They are too heavy for you. He invites you to take His yoke. He wants to team up with you, so you no longer bear the heavy load alone. He wants to join forces with you so you can defeat the enemy. It is His intention for you to be with Him throughout eternity, so He has linked His heart and life to yours.

Jesus invites you to unburden yourself and hand your cares over to Him because He can handle them. His humility and willingness to subject Himself to death on the cross will redeem you and provide access to all your needs, which can only be found in Him. He tells you His yoke is easy and His burden is light. A burden is a small everyday thing that weighs us down. It is like a school bag, which will not collapse when you adjust it over your shoulders. You believe you can handle it alone, so you take it without asking God for help.

A yoke, however, requires assistance. It is more than you can lift and carry on your own, so Jesus gives you the solution. He invites you to yoke up with Him! Come to Him because He has rest for you. He wants your soul to find peace in Him. As you go to Jesus, you discover not only is the burden lifted, but He also fills you with peace and hope; envelops you in love; and allows you to see the joy-filled life He has planned for you. He has only the best for you, and you can trust Him to handle all your concerns.

He is willing and available to lift and carry every burden from your shoulders.

The baggage is not yours to carry – dump it!
You can trust God to take care of it.

7

AT THE THRONE

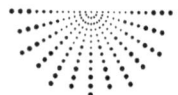

$\mathcal{I}$n the previous chapters, I shared with you what God does in the waiting room of life. In this chapter, I want to focus on the benefits you gain as you prioritize spending time with God in the throne room. This is where you get to know Him deeper and more meaningfully. To develop this relationship with the Lord, you must steal away with Him. Schedule time so you can meet with Him to hear His plans and purposes for your life.

The time you spend in the throne room begins remodeling you into the image of God's Son. In this place, God begins a deep work in your heart and teaches you to depend on Him. Some of us may struggle with trusting and relying on God because we may not have had a good example of this while growing up. If your father was not in the home, it might have caused you not to be able to relate to God as Father. Since you did not have a good earthly example of how a father provides and protects his children, you may see God as you do your earthly father.

There are others whose dads were in the home but were abusive. As a result, you may not clearly understand God the Father is a loving and compassionate Father.

You may not know He will never abuse nor abandon you but will take care of you and see you through all your difficulties. Sometimes we may blame God for the abuses we have suffered; therefore, we do not desire an intimate relationship with Him. There are still some people whose dads were physically present but emotionally absent. They cannot talk with God about their needs because their earthly fathers did not teach them how to share.

If you fall into any of these categories, God invites you to spend quality time with Him so you can get to know His love and deep regard for you. God is unlike our earthly fathers, even if you had a good one. He is your ultimate parent and loves you way beyond what an earthly parent feels for you. God hurts when you hurt, and He weeps with you in your brokenness. King David understood the depth of God's love and compassion for him because he constantly sought refuge in the presence of God.

O LORD, thou hast searched me, and known me. Thou knowest my downsitting and mine uprising; thou understandest my thought afar off. Thou compassest my path and my lying down, and art acquainted with all my ways. For there is not a word in my tongue, but, lo, O LORD, thou knowest it altogether. Thou hast beset me behind and before, and laid thine hand upon me. Such knowledge is too wonderful for me; it is high, I cannot attain

unto it. Whither shall I go from thy Spirit? Or whither shall I flee from thy presence? If I ascend up into heaven, thou art there: if I make my bed in hell, behold, thou art there. If I take the wings of the morning, and dwell in the uttermost parts of the sea; even there shall thy hand lead me, and thy right hand shall hold me.
Psalm 139:1-10 (KJV)

As I read this scripture, I am reminded of how often I have tried to avoid the deep work God wanted to do in my life. Despite my efforts, I still spend time in the waiting room and then in the throne room. It is hard to allow the Lord to search and examine our hearts because we do not want to expose ourselves to His scrutiny. You need to remember that God knows it all and sees it all. Nothing is ever hidden from Him, so you may as well allow Him to come in and do the work that will bring about His greater glory in your life.

In the waiting room, God invites you to be yourself. He cannot work with you if you try to be someone else. You are a pearl of great price to God, so He is not trying to change you because you have no value. God desires to polish you so that the radiance of who you are will shine brighter and brighter. After this transforming work, God can be seen in your life. When others see His reflection in you, they will also know Him.

While in the waiting room, I tried to find an easier way out because I did not want to examine myself too closely. Who knows, maybe I was afraid of what I would see! It seemed as though I often ended up in the same situation. It finally dawned on me God was after something buried deep in my heart. He allowed these situations into my life to get my attention.

I was unemployed several times, which plunged me into another season in the waiting room. I knew God wanted to do a work in me, and I was unwilling to yield or surrender because I knew the work would be intense and require dying to my selfish ways and desires, and I was not ready to surrender.

In my book, **"Called and Chosen for Destiny,"** I shared how God got my attention as I was headed into the wilderness, like the Israelites. He asked why I believed I deserved to be promoted in His Kingdom when I continued to fail the tests that came my way.

He reminded me that in school; I would not pass when I failed a grade; He most definitely would not promote me when I kept failing. Yet, I was still unwilling for Him to do a work in my heart.

What did I fear? The answer is simple – I had not learned to trust God. I was afraid He would do something in me I did not want or send me places I did not want to go. We struggle with letting God have His way with us because we think He will harm us somehow. Again, we are comparing Him with our earthly fathers, and since some of them were untrustworthy, we believe God is the same way.

Time at the Throne is designed to look deeply into our hearts, assess what is there, determine if we depend on God, and then decide if we can trust Him to do everything He promises in His Word.

I love Psalm 139 because King David gives us great insight into who God is, where He is, and His knowledge of things far too wonderful for us to comprehend. While we are busy trying to avoid the waiting room, we do not realize part of the time spent there will be Throne time when we meet God face-to-face.

David asked some crucial questions we must ask today. "Is there any place we can go to escape God's Spirit?" "Where can we flee from God's presence?" David tells us if we ascend into heaven, God is there because it is His home. If we intend to make our beds in hell, God is there too!

Is David saying God lives in hell? Not! He is saying there is knowledge God exists even in that dark place. Those sharing this space with the devil and his angels have discovered too late that God and heaven are real. They realize, to their dismay, that when they were alive and determined to live apart from Him by ignoring His Son, their desire was granted. Now, they are in torment and understand those who accepted Jesus are enjoying the benefits of being in God's presence. They know God exists!

David tells us that if he had wings and could fly away in the morning to the uttermost part of the sea, God's hand would still be upon him. King David is telling us that there is no place where God does not exist. God is everywhere; He is in everything, and there is no avoiding Him. The occasions I ran away from the Throne and from the work God wanted to do in my heart were not fruitful times. God has a way of pursuing, wooing, and drawing us to Himself. Because He has a plan and a calling for each life, He will keep pursuing you until He wins you over and completes the work in your heart.

Throne time must be embraced because this time

cements a deeper personal relationship with the Lord. It develops a deep level of trust in God. God uses this time to fashion and mold you into the image of His beautiful Son. Why? So, He can bless your life with the abundant blessings He has reserved for you.

Jesus also spent time in the waiting room. After He was baptized, the Spirit led Him into the wilderness to be tempted by the devil. We saw His heart was firmly established in God, and he won and prevailed over Satan (Matthew 4). During the time Jesus in the Garden of Gethsemane asked to be released from death on the cross, but He surrendered His will to God so He could die for us and accomplish God's will for mankind. He knew after His death; that God would raise Him from the dead; therefore, He went to hell and took back the keys of death and hell that the devil had stolen from Adam and Eve.

Jesus died to redeem and return us to our rightful place of dominion and authority over the earth. His time of testing, willingness to surrender to God, and life given in exchange for ours, shows us time spent at the Throne is worth the rewards. Jesus is now exalted and is seated at the right hand of God.

Let me share one more scripture with you to drive this point home.

I will bless the LORD, who hath given me counsel: my reins also instruct me in the night seasons. I have set the LORD always before me: because he is at my right hand, I shall not be moved. Therefore my heart is glad, and my glory rejoiceth: my flesh also shall rest in hope. For thou wilt not leave my soul in hell; neither

wilt thou suffer thine Holy One to see corruption. Thou wilt show me the path of life: in thy presence is fullness of joy; at thy right hand there are pleasures for evermore.
Psalm 16:7-11(KJV)

This scripture shows us the results of time spent in the waiting room and God's Throne room. You will discover God's blueprint, the path He has mapped out for you, and His plan for your life. His path always leads to the correct destination, and you will find deep fulfillment in God's presence. You will find the fullness of joy, life, strength, and personal fulfillment in the time spent at the Throne of God. You will discover what pleasure there is in God's presence. God loves His children and has created all the beauty in the world for us to have and enjoy. He knows us well and has keen insight into how to provide enjoyment for each of us. He knows what will bless, encourage, and bring joy to our hearts.

In God's presence, your pleasure will not be for a season but forever – time without end. Throughout eternity, you will overflow with joy because He dispenses it to those willing to draw near, allowing Him to have His way in their hearts and lives.

Are you running from Throne time? There is no need -- God will unfold a great plan as you spend time with Him. He is trustworthy and will finish His work in you.

Decide to meet Him at the Throne today!

8

REFORMING CHARACTER

*W*e have heard a lot about our character over the years, especially regarding how we serve God and others. Character is your manner, nature, disposition, temperament, and personality. God is always working on our character so that we can be a blessing in His kingdom.

Part of the time spent in the waiting rooms of life is when God works on transforming your character. You may ask why your character needs to be changed; because Adam and Eve sinned, we, as their offspring, were born with the same sinful nature as theirs.

The scripture says we are shaped in iniquity, and in sin did our mother conceive us (Psalm 51:5). As a result of Adam and Eve's sin, you and I have been patterned or molded after their likeness. We have been born in sin, so by our very nature, we are conditioned to do that which is wrong, immoral, and wicked. This is the reason God put another plan in place to redeem us. The Bible records Jesus as coming and rescuing us so we would not be eternally lost.

In the waiting room, God is remaking and reforming our character so we can reflect His image and live as He always intended us to live. In transforming us, God goes deep into the core of our hearts to uproot things that are not a reflection of His nature, character, and the person we are meant to be.

Our environment, homes, and even some events in our family life will cause some of us to be hurtful and wicked. We will do and speak evil to others; most of the time, we do not appear to be fully cognizant of what we are doing. We fail to realize that evil is always present, as there are good things in the world. Our nature is molded by the things we allow to enter our hearts and lives.

In our hearts is a desire put there by God to do the things that are right and godly, but another nature is at war with our good intentions. As we try to do what is right, the other nature pulls us along a more destructive path. It is as if we are in a tug-of-war, and whatever is deeply rooted in us will be what wins. If God is not allowed to deal with the severe issues in our hearts and reform our character, we will fail to maximize the life He desires us to have.

Let us look at an example of what happens when we do not allow God to reform or remake our character.

Now when Jesus was in Bethany, in the house of Simon the leper, there came unto him a woman having an alabaster box of very precious ointment, and poured it on His head, as he sat at meat. But when his disciples saw it, they had indignation, saying, To

what purpose is this waste? For this ointment might have been sold for much, and given to the poor. When Jesus understood it, he said unto them, Why trouble ye the woman? For she hath wrought a good work upon me. For ye have the poor always with you; but me ye have not always. For in that she hath poured this ointment on my body, she did it for my burial. Verily I say unto you, wheresoever this gospel shall be preached in the whole world, there shall also this, that this woman hath done, be told for a memorial of her. Then one of the twelve, called Judas Iscariot, went unto the chief priests, and said unto them, What will ye give me, and I will deliver him unto you? And they covenanted with Him for thirty pieces of silver. And from that time he sought opportunity to betray him.
Matthew 26:6-16 (KJV)

Judas! How many of you are familiar with this name? You know him as the betrayer of Jesus, and Judas was the man who sold Jesus for thirty pieces of silver. He was the treasurer and had been stealing from Jesus. I am sure if this woman had put the money in the treasury Judas would have felt much better about her because he would have stolen a portion of it for his use. However, he did not get the opportunity because she poured her best offering on the Master.

Jesus chose Judas to be one of His disciples. He oversaw the money used to run the ministry. You may ask why Jesus would give him the assignment knowing his nature. The answer is we all can choose right from wrong. We will always be allowed to walk with integrity and make better decisions with our lives; this was Judas' opportunity, and he missed it. He was part of Jesus' inner circle, this elite group of disciples, and he had intimate knowledge of the Master, but he did not learn from Him.

The scripture above shows the disciples' anger about the perfume poured on Jesus. The disciples failed to understand that this woman was preparing Jesus for His death and burial. Many of the disciples were angry because they thought the woman was being wasteful. When Jesus rebuked them and explained what she was doing, they relented, yielded their hearts, and moved forward, but not Judas.

As you study the scriptures, it becomes evident Judas' character needed transformation. He was a thief and did not have the best intentions toward Jesus and the assignment He was given. You may ask, "But why would Jesus choose such a person for His team?" The answer is simple – because He loved him, and in His presence, Judas' life could have been changed and transformed.

Judas could have experienced a complete transformation not only in his character but also in his life. He could have received and enjoyed the forgiveness available to him, but he did not seek to be forgiven. Jesus also understood that for Him to die and rescue us, someone had to betray Him, so God allowed Judas to be a part of His team. I also believe God intended for Judas to see all the miracles Jesus performed to get a glimpse of His Kingdom assignment. Judas' character and life could have changed after catching this glimpse of the Kingdom.

I have often wondered if Judas realized Jesus would be crucified. I have concluded he thought they would flog and jail Him, but I do not believe he thought beyond that to foresee the actual consequences of his betrayal.

He intended to make a few quick dollars and still have access to the Master. He failed to remember the hatred some Jewish leaders had toward Jesus and that they were looking for an opportunity to destroy Him. How Judas could have missed the number of times the Jews tried to trap Jesus and how often Jesus could not walk among them openly is unfathomable. Judas was totally into himself. He was lost in his own needs and desires and did not comprehend the Jewish leaders hated Jesus because He was God's Son. They refused to believe and serve Him. Judas failed to see that some of the religious leaders' intentions toward his Master were for harm, not good. If he had not failed to realize this, he might have made better decisions about being such a significant part of Jesus' crucifixion.

Judas walked, ate, prayed, fellowshipped, and fed the many thousands with Jesus. He had seen the food multiplied and witnessed the signs, wonders, and miracles, yet his heart had not changed, and his character remained the same. How could he have witnessed the great things he saw and remained the same? Why was his heart so hardened? How is it that God's presence and power did not change him? The answer is simple. It is the same way that Jesus has touched and changed the hearts and lives of our loved ones, yet we are still not moved to change.

We have witnessed His healing miracles in our lives, experienced His forgiveness, felt His transforming power at work in our midst, and yet some of our hearts are still hardened. As a result, like Judas, we do not experience breaking and remolding our hearts so God can accomplish what He desires in our lives.

At the last supper with the disciples, Jesus told them one of them would betray Him. They were all astonished and saddened to hear this announcement and began to ask Him who it was. Jesus said, "The one who dips his hand with Me in the dip" would be the one to betray Him. Judas also asked the Lord if he was the one, and Jesus affirmed it, but Judas did not repent or turn away from the evil in his heart.

Judas stayed for the entire meal and took communion with them. He ate the bread representing the broken body of Jesus and drank the wine representing the shedding of His blood, yet he turned, walked away, and betrayed Him.

His heart must have been calloused to have shared this last feast with the Master and not be moved to change his ways. The pull of financial gain was stronger than the desire to stay close to Jesus. Some have been tempted by things that pull us away from the Master even after intimate fellowship with Him. The great news is you have a chance to return to Him and be forgiven. After Judas left, Jesus and the disciples walked to the Garden of Gethsemane. While Jesus was praying, Judas sold his Lord.

Before bringing the priests and elders to arrest Jesus, Judas told them the one he kissed would be Jesus. The priests were to arrest Him and hold Him fast. Judas greeted Jesus calling Him Master, and then kissed Him. This kiss demonstrated his close relationship and bond with Jesus. Jesus shows us the forgiveness and love in His heart toward Judas. He said to him, *"Friend, wherefore art thou come?"* Jesus was asking, *"Judas, my friend, why are you here?"* How tender Jesus' words were to Judas.

In those words was another chance for Judas to change his ways. Judas could have easily said, "Master, I have sinned and need your forgiveness." The Jews would have still realized this was Jesus and could have arrested Him without Judas' help. How different Judas' life would have been, and how wonderfully reformed his character would have become. His testimony would have been a beacon of hope to the many generations following him. Judas had spent three years living in close quarters with Jesus, and in the final analysis, his character had not been changed into the image of the Son. He had many opportunities to transform his heart and life, but he let each slip through his fingers.

In the previous paragraph, I told you I did not believe Judas fully understood the price Jesus would pay for his betrayal. The devil, the deceiver, and the liar only told lies to Judas, and he believed them. In Matthew chapter twenty-seven, Judas realized Jesus was condemned to die. He was remorseful and tried to return the thirty pieces of silver to the priests and the elders. He said to them, "I have sinned, for I have betrayed an innocent man." They told him they did not care, so he threw the coins down, walked out, and hanged himself.

Judas realized, too late, that he had missed his opportunity. He recognized that greed had caused him to sell his Master, and in the end, it was not worth it. God leads us into the waiting room, to work on our character so we will not sell out Jesus.

This work is to keep us living in a way that will not displease or bring shame to His Kingdom. It is to mold us into the image of God's precious Son, so we will do what He says to do and go where He says to go. God gives us the same opportunities He gave Jesus - to obey and follow His commandments. The Bible records Jesus as only doing what He sees the Father doing, and the Holy Spirit only does what He sees Jesus doing. Therefore, you and I must only do what the Holy Spirit says. As we follow His lead, we will be transformed into the image of God's Son.

As I conclude this chapter, my eyes are filled with tears because of the opportunities I have missed to be pleasing to the Son. I have not always trusted Him as I should, but God is faithful, and you can trust Him. Daily, I pray for God to help me trust Him more and keep me from doing things that will bring shame to His kingdom and His name.

Let this be your prayer as well, that you will always strive to please the Lord. As you do so, remember He will begin a work in you that will ultimately transform your character and life into His image and likeness.

9
FACE-TO-FACE

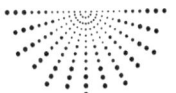

*H*ow many of you cannot wait to see Jesus face-to-face? I am like you in this because I, too, long to behold His beautiful face. This does not mean we do not desire to live our lives fully or finish the assignments. We simply want to spend time with Him thanking Him for all He has done. He is the reason we live! What joy and continual fellowship we will have in His presence.

In the waiting room, it is possible to develop such deep intimacy with God that you will experience what Adam and Eve experienced in the Garden of Eden. They shared a level of communion and oneness with Him that was beyond belief. God met with them face-to-face as He walked and talked with them each day in the Garden, in the cool of the day. They communed, fellowshipped, and basked in one another's presence. How beautiful it must have been to hear God calling their names to let them know it was time for their intimate discussions. God will do the same for you if that is a desire of your heart. When you long after God with all your heart, He will come and meet with you face-to-face.

In these encounters, your life will be enriched, and you will have boundless joy because in His presence is fullness of joy (Psalm 16:11). Some people will feel they cannot get enough time in His presence and desire to spend more time with Him so His mercy and love can saturate them. In your face-to-face meetings with the Lord, you will have opportunities to share the deep longings of your soul with Him. You will find He is available, listening, and ready to grant your desires. You will encounter Him in a new, profound, and powerful way because He desires you to know Him intimately.

After allowing Him to do the work He does in the waiting room, there is nothing that will hinder you from deeper intimacy with Him. In the waiting room, He is stripping you so you can get closer and closer to Him. When He completes His work in your heart, you will have the desire to go deeper. I long for more and more and more of God! How about you? Do you long for Him to completely take over your life? If this is your heart's cry, you will have divine encounters with Him.

Abraham, our forefather, met the Lord face-to-face, and his life was transformed. I encourage you to read the entire chapter to see how God spoke with him as he met the Lord at his home entrance.

The Lord appeared again to Abraham near the oak grove belonging to Mamre. One day Abraham was sitting at the entrance to his tent during the hottest part of the day. He looked up and noticed three men standing nearby. When he saw them,

he ran to meet them and welcomed them, bowing low to the ground. "My lord," he said, "If it pleases you, stop here for a while. Rest in the shade of this tree while water is brought to wash your feet. And since you've honored your servant with this visit, let me prepare some food to refresh you before continuing your journey." "All right," they said. "Do as you have said." So Abraham ran back to the tent and said to Sarah, "Hurry! Get three large measures of your best flour, knead it into dough, and bake some bread." Then Abraham ran out to the herd and chose a tender calf and gave it to his servant, who quickly prepared it. When the food was ready, Abraham took some yogurt and milk and the roasted meat, and he served it to the men. As they ate, Abraham waited on them in the shade of the trees. "Where is Sarah, your wife?" The visitors asked. "She's inside the tent," Abraham replied. Then one of them said, "I will return to you about this time next year, and your wife, Sarah, will have a son!" Sarah was listening to this conversation from the tent. Abraham and Sarah were both very old by this time, and Sarah was long past the age of having children. So she laughed silently to herself and said, "How could a worn-out woman like me enjoy such pleasure, especially when my master – my husband - is also so old?" Then the LORD said to Abraham, "Why did Sarah laugh? Why did she say, 'Can an old woman like me have a baby?' Is anything too hard for the LORD? I will return about this time next year, and Sarah will have a son."
Genesis 18:1-14 (NLT)

Abraham had a face-to-face encounter with the Lord while sitting in the tent's doorway. The Lord was on a mission to destroy the city of Sodom because of the people's sins, and He stopped to talk with Abraham. Abraham's nephew Lot lived in Sodom.

Abraham immediately recognized these men were not typical visitors, and he bowed down in worship. Abraham knew he was in the presence of the Lord, and he honored Him. He quickly went about preparing refreshments for them. Although the Lord was on His way to destroy the wayward people in Sodom, He made time to stop and speak with His friend, whose heart was steadfast toward Him.

This is the same love God has for His children; no matter how busy He is, He will always make time for you. The Lord sat down and fellowshipped with Abraham, giving him a great promise in his old age. They were promised a son when Abraham and Sarah met the Lord face-to-face. Nine months later, Sarah gave birth to a son and named him "Laughter" because God filled them with joy when He fulfilled His promise. Each time you meet with the Lord, you will come away with a richer life because He always blesses those who seek after Him.

As you continue reading this chapter, you discover the Lord decided not to hide His plan to destroy Sodom from Abraham. This decision came because of Abraham's relationship with God. He was not a distant friend but one who stayed close to God. God chose to share His plans with Abraham because Abraham had continual fellowship and communion with Him. The same holds for you as well. When you continually fellowship with God, He will share His heart and desires.

Sodom's sins were so flagrant the Lord decided to come down to see if it was as bad as He had heard. Think about that statement for a moment. The Lord Himself came down from Heaven to see if what He had heard about the sin of Sodom was as great as He had heard. It appears as if the Lord could not believe what He heard because it was unbelievable. Who told Him about the sins? Could it have been the angels who were assigned to that region? Whoever it was, it was enough to move the God of Heaven to intervene.

Abraham was allowed to question the Lord about His decision and asked if He would destroy the righteous and the wicked together. Abraham challenged the Lord about His plan for Sodom. Abraham said to the Lord, "Surely you won't do such a thing, destroying the righteous along with the wicked?"

Remember, Abraham's nephew was in the city. (This happens in your face-to-face encounters with the Lord – you can reason with Him, share your concerns, and hear His heart on a matter). The Lord heard Abraham's concerns and told him if He found fifty righteous people, He would not destroy the city. Abraham asked more of the Lord because he knew He would not find fifty righteous people in Sodom.

Abraham continued and asked the Lord not to destroy the city if He could find forty-five, forty, thirty, or twenty righteous people. He asked the Lord not to be angry with him and asked for one last request, "Suppose only ten righteous are found?" and the Lord replied, "Then I will not destroy it for the sake of ten."

The Bible does not mention how many people lived in Sodom during this time; archaeologists have estimated there were between 600-1200 people. Incredibly, God could not find ten righteous people in this small community. Abraham was bold with his pleas to save the people because he had an intimate relationship with God. God responded to his requests because of their relationship. Abraham could talk intimately with the Lord, who listened, heard, and cared about his request. God does not desire to destroy anyone but wants everyone to repent and have a relationship with Him.

Unfortunately, Sodom was destroyed because the Lord could not find ten righteous people there. How is it possible there were not ten righteous people in that city? The one righteous man who lived among them, Abraham's nephew Lot, apparently did not display the presence and power of God to them. He lived among them, married one of their daughters, and produced children but did not affect them enough to make a difference in their lives.

Before we judge him too harshly, let us examine ourselves. How many neighbors, co-workers, friends, family members, etc., know about our devotion to God? Have we lived our lives so others are drawn to Him?

How about sharing how His power has transformed us into a life of holiness? Many of us miss opportunities to introduce others to Christ. We are afraid of being rejected or unwilling to step out of our comfort zone to share our testimony.

Twenty-four years after Abram and Lot began their journey, the Lord changed Abram's name to Abraham, giving him the covenant promise of a son. Not long after, God appeared to Abraham and shared His plans to destroy Sodom. Lot had over twenty-four years to change the hearts of at least ten people, yet only His wife and daughters were saved. Not even his daughters' fiancées were saved—what a wasted life.

Abraham's nephew and his family escaped with their lives. Lot's wife lost hers on the way because she longed for what she had left behind, even after the Lord warned them not to look back.

I hope you realize from this story that you have divine opportunities to make a difference in many lives as you continue to meet the Lord face-to-face. Not only will He change and transform your life, but He will give you opportunities to help Him change, transform, and impact the lives of others. It is God's great desire that we make disciples of men, and He wants us to introduce the lost to Jesus Christ's saving power. You and I have been given a wonderful gift, a relationship with the Savior of the universe, and He is a gift worth sharing. Only He can change a life, a community, a city, a nation, and a world. When we introduce people to the Savior, He will meet with them face-to-face as He meets with you.

As Lot reviewed his life, I wondered how regretful he may have been because of his lost opportunities.

Let us not live our lives regretting the opportunities that we may have missed to introduce others to Jesus. Begin today to proclaim His goodness to everyone you meet. Remember, the Bible says that some plant the seeds, others water them, but it is God who gives the increase
(1 Corinthian 3:5-7).

In your face-to-face meetings with God, ask Him to help you reach the lost for Him, and He will enable and empower you.

VICTORY IN THE WAITING

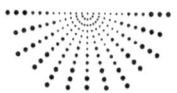

*A*ll of us love to hear the sound of victory. Whether it is a victory song, a shout of joy, or a heartfelt cry, it tells us something—we win. We long to hear these sounds in the waiting room because they mean we have overcome the struggles, and great blessings await us. Getting to the place of victory has not been an easy journey for many people. In some cases, there have been many tears, prayers, frustrations, and even times of hopelessness. Through all of this, we have had no option but to wait.

In the waiting, we had to battle hard to keep standing and pressing forward when nothing seemed to work in our favor. During the waiting season, and while in the waiting room, many things will be birthed in us. We will either succeed or experience defeat. The things birthed during the waiting room season can be a platform for life, either lived for the glory of God or glorifying self and even the enemy. While waiting, some will mature in their faith; others will choose not to pursue a deeper relationship with God because the waiting is too painful. Still, others will decide the struggles to get to victory are not worth it and will choose to live life on their terms. Whatever your choice, you will reap each decision's blessings or consequences. You must choose wisely.

Remember, God does not waste a single thing in our life, so if He allows you to be in this waiting season, there is a great reward at the end. As you are strengthened and remodeled in the waiting season, you can come away with more solid faith and a more incredible testimony. You will grow and mature to a higher degree than you ever dreamed possible, and your Christian walk will bring glory to God. This occurs because whatever is in us is exposed, tried, and refined in the fires of adversities. As we go through the struggles, many things in our hearts will be made more visible, not only to ourselves but to others who are watching our walk of faith. One thing is for sure—your victory is assured. Your assurance comes from knowing Jesus has already won the victory on your behalf. Jesus is waiting for you to go and gather the blessings He has left along the way as you journey toward your destination.

Victory in the waiting means we are connected to the Source, God. Your connection to Him will always produce an abundant harvest in your life. I have served the Lord for most of my life and can tell you I have spent most of it in the waiting room. It began in my teenage years as I struggled to find my place and understand what God wanted for my life. I worked on my family relationships, health, and school. When I began college at eighteen, I struggled to stay afloat financially. After finishing college, I was hired by a company and moved to Houston, Texas. The company began to struggle financially a year later, and my paychecks started bouncing. Here I was in a new city and now jobless.

Through all these challenges, I have been frustrated, discouraged, apathetic, mad at God and others, and ready to quit. God has helped me keep waiting and trusting Him. I failed to realize even though life was difficult, God was molding and reshaping my heart so He could use me more effectively in His Kingdom.

My waiting room experiences did not last for only a few months or a few years. Some of them have lasted for decades, and in some instances, I still await God to give me victory in certain areas. One of my greatest lessons in the waiting season is how to trust God in all things. Because the journey has been long and arduous, sometimes I have struggled with trusting that God knows best and that he is not allowing me to travel this road without rhyme or reason. With each small victory, God has shown me He can be trusted even when I cannot trace His hands at work in my life.

As I sit and write this book, I can assure you joy does come in the morning. Over the last ten years, God has begun to unfold His plans in my life, and I now see the waiting season as preparation for His destiny for me to fulfill. During the waiting season, God processed my heart to know if I would be a vessel of honor in His court. Could I be trusted with the assignment of speaking into the hearts and lives of His people? Would I be faithful to go where He leads? We all have plans for our lives; sometimes, they are not God's plans for us. God is now using me to minister His Word in many places. In addition, He has birthed a desire in my heart to care for those considered the least, not only in the United States but worldwide.

When God first told me He wanted me to do mission work, take the Gospel of the Kingdom to other nations, and provide humanitarian aid, my reaction was like this: I hate the heat and bugs. I was not jumping for joy at first, but after many mission outreaches and thousands of lives saved, changed, helped, and healed, I can't imagine doing anything else. In the waiting room, God aligned my heart to His heart and plans, so I would willingly follow where He leads.

I developed stamina, faithfulness, trust, confidence, and hope during the tough times so I could walk in the assignments He gave me. I have had to trust Him to provide for each mission trip. He has never failed me. Without those trying seasons in the waiting room, my life would be less meaningful because I would not have begun to accomplish what God planned for me. Although I await many things from the Lord, the journey is becoming easier. The journey for you will also become easier as you allow God to do the work He desires to do in your heart.

When I consider victory in the waiting, I expect God to amaze me with His goodness and wonders. Victory for you is knowing God is the one who is in control of your life and destiny. As a result, you cannot lose, nor will you fail. God's victory for your life may not look as you expect it to when it arrives. You must be open and flexible with what God has mapped out for you.

Let's look at what happened when Jesus came to earth, and the people expected Him to establish His earthly Kingdom.

Jesus said, "My kingdom is not of this world. If it were, my servants would fight to prevent my arrest by the Jewish leaders. But now my kingdom is from another place." "You are a king, then!" said Pilate. Jesus answered, "You say that I am a king. In fact, the reason I was born and came into the world is to testify to the truth. Everyone on the side of truth listens to me." "What is truth?" retorted Pilate. With this he went out again to the Jews gathered there and said, "I find no basis for a charge against him."
John 18:36-38

One of the challenges Jesus faced was dealing with those who thought He would establish an earthly kingdom. Even some of the disciples expected this. The mother of James and John went to Jesus and asked for a special favor – that her sons would sit, one on His right hand and the other on His left hand.

They believed Jesus was here to establish an earthly kingdom (Matthew 20:20-22). The other disciples were not happy with this development. They had yet to learn that Jesus was not trying to establish His earthly Kingdom; that would be many years into the future. In the above scripture, when Jesus was brought before Pilate, Pilate asked Him about His Kingdom. The Jews had informed Pilate that Jesus believed Himself to be a King. As a result, they were expecting Him to establish His throne. I think this was the Jewish leaders' underlying fear; Jesus was going to establish an earthly kingdom, and this would be a disaster for them. Therefore, they plotted to get rid of the King. They failed to realize they fulfilled what God had sent Jesus to earth to accomplish – freedom for us who were slaves of the enemy and sin. Jesus' death provided us a way back to God the Father.

Since the people expected Jesus to establish His kingdom on earth, they did not understand His death or believe in His resurrection. Like us, they needed to get to know Jesus to see His purpose for their lives and how He planned to fulfill those purposes. I encourage you to let go of any false expectations, spend time with God, and discover what He has planned for you and your future. Do not be like the Jews who could not see that Jesus' Kingdom was far greater, more eternal, and everlasting than their expectations. One day, Jesus will return to reestablish His earthly Kingdom; everyone will know about it when He does.

As you are in the seasons of waiting, I challenge you to expect God to move suddenly. If the things you pray for align with His plans for your life, they will come to pass if you do not give up. Your expectation and hope in Him will be fulfilled because He never fails. Much joy and happiness come from walking in the fullness of His promises for you.

Over the last several years, it has been my joy and fulfillment to begin walking and living in the destiny God has mapped out for my life. Although I have spent many years waiting for several promises to manifest, I am now enjoying the blessings of seeing God move with great power. He is opening doors no man can shut and allowing us to be His hands and feet to those in need. I expect soon we will see an unprecedented move of God, not only in our lives but in the lives of others as well. Your victory is assured; all you must do is continue to walk in faith. You will be victorious and get to the great destiny God has mapped out for your future.

I hope and pray that your relationship with God, Jesus, and the Holy Spirit has deepened due to the time you have spent reading this book and will deepen even more from the time you spend in God's "Waiting Room." Do not be anxious about this time – it is well worth it, and you can trust God to meet you in the waiting room and to do deep work in your heart.

How do you trust God in the waiting? There is no formula for trusting – you decide to trust and do it. It is a day-by-day choice, an act of your will to trust Him each step of the way. You will learn how to trust and obey only Him in the waiting room. Jesus is ready and waiting for you in the waiting room. Are you ready to meet Him there?

11
SCRIPTURES FOR ENCOURAGEMENT

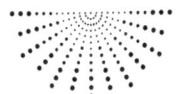

But they that wait upon the LORD shall renew their strength; they shall mount up with wings as eagles; they shall run, and not be weary; and they shall walk, and not faint.
Isaiah 40:31 (KJV)

Come unto me, all ye that labor and are heavy laden, and I will give you rest. Take my yoke upon you, and learn of me; for I am meek and lowly in heart: and ye shall find rest unto your souls. For my yoke is easy, and my burden is light.
Matthew 11:28-30 (KJV)

And let us not be weary in well doing: for in due season we shall reap, if we faint not.
Galatians 6:9 (KJV)

Therefore, my dear brothers and sisters, stand firm. Let nothing move you. Always give yourselves fully to the work of the Lord, because you know that your labor in the Lord is not in vain.
1 Corinthians 15:58 (NIV)

For we walk by faith, not by sight.
2 Corinthians 5:7 (KJV)

For our light affliction, which is but for a moment, worketh for us a far more exceeding and eternal weight of glory; while we look not at the things which are seen, but at the things which are not seen: for the things which are seen are temporal; but the things which are not seen are eternal.
2 Corinthians 4:17-18 (KJV)

Not that I speak in respect of want: for I have learned, in whatsoever state I am, therewith to be content.
Philippians 4:11 (KJV)

But my God shall supply all your need according to his riches in glory by Christ Jesus.
Philippians 4:19 (KJV)

Rejoice in the Lord always: and again I say, Rejoice.
Philippians 4:4 (KJV)

"For my thoughts are not your thoughts, neither are your ways my ways," declares the LORD. "As the heavens are higher than the earth, so are my ways higher than your ways and my thoughts than your thoughts. As the rain and snow come down from heaven, and do not return to it without watering the earth and making it bud and flourish, so that it yields seed for the sower and bread for the eater, so is my word that goes out from my mouth: It will not return to me empty, but will accomplish what I desire and achieve the purpose for which I sent it. You will go out in joy and be led forth in peace.
Isaiah 55:8-12a (NIV)

God is not a man who lies, or a son of man who changes His mind. Does He speak and not act, or promise and not fulfill?
Numbers 23:19 (HCSB)

May these scriptures encourage and enrich you in the waiting season!

12

PRAYER OF SALVATION

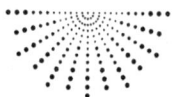

*J*esus, I invite You to come into my heart; forgive me of my sins; cleanse me from all unrighteousness, and make Your home in me. You promise if I confess my sins, You will be faithful to forgive me. I humbly confess them now and ask Your forgiveness and pardon. I invite You to make Your home securely in my heart from this day forward; in Jesus' name, I pray.

Amen!

ABOUT THE AUTHOR

Joan Murray is committed to helping people discover their destinies. She is the founder and CEO of Joan Murray Ministries and Seeds of Hope Worldwide Missions. Joan is dedicated to teaching, training, equipping, and helping people with various life struggles.

Joan is a minister, Bible teacher, author, and missionary. She has traveled extensively throughout the United States and internationally sharing the gospel message and serving the needs of the oppressed. Joan currently resides in Houston, Texas.

If you would like to know more about Joan Murray Ministries or Seeds of Hope Worldwide Missions, please get in touch with us at:

Joan Murray Ministries & Seeds Of Hope Worldwide
Missions
26340 FM 1736
Waller, TX 77848
281-398-2501
email: jmmcontactus@gmail.com
website: www.jemmuniquegift.com
website: www.joanmurrayministries.org

**Changing Lives Through the Power and Truth of God's
Word.**

www.ingramcontent.com/pod-product-compliance
Lightning Source LLC
Chambersburg PA
CBHW070927120626
46546CB00004B/1367